T0380772

To order additional copies of this book, contact:
Xlibris LLC
1-888-795-4274
www.Xlibris.com
Orders@Xlibris.com

"Hare" 'n There

'N

There

Adventures of Rosie Rabbit

Rosie in Paris

Story, Poem & Cover by: Diane Herak

TABLE OF CONTENTS

DEDICATION

This book is dedicated to my beloved family, my two Daughters, Deborah, and Amy, my six Sons, Peter, Wally, David, Mark, Dale and Christopher. To each of their spouses, or very significant other, my 17 joyous Grand-Children, and one Great Grandson.

The many children's books I've read throughout the years, and the many places I've had the pleasure of traveling, inspired me to put my thoughts and experiences in books.

I am confident that the spirits around me will guide my ·fingers over the keys…and will connect in my mind, so I will recall details, perhaps long forgotten, that I'd like to share.

My sister, Rosemary is important in my dedication, as she has influenced my creativity of painting and writing. She raised me when we had no one.

Last, but surely not least my appreciation and gratitude to my soul-mate and constant companion for many years…my Jimmy K, who always supports my projects , my ideas, my life.

INTRODUCTION

Rosie Rabbit is about to bring you wonderful adventures about the places she travels. She will tell you of her incredible visits in many parts of the world, and also in The United States.

The series of books will be fun reading and will act as very interesting Social Studies. Each story will begin with a poem about the point of destination and a map showing the location.

Now and then, Rosie may be in a bit of danger, or find herself confused. However, our traveling bunny in a happy one with a good attitude and therefore always manages to get back on track.

In this, her first adventure, she spends time in the beautiful city of Paris. While she wanders through the streets and sees the amazing places, she is not alone because of all the friendly people she meets along the way. She wants to visit all of the sights that she was told about, and wants to share it with you.

Along with traveling, Rosie loves healthy eating, good work-outs and especially loves children. She would like to set an example to all who read about her adventures.

Map Poem of Paris-by Diane Herak

On this map of France, Paris is marked by a Fleur-de-lis. This is a popular symbol throughout France.

Fleur means flower and lis means lily… therefore it is "Flower of the Lily."

Paris

Paris, I'm in Paris, Oh joyful am I,

From the Tower, called Eiffel, many clouds do pass by.

I shall cruise up the Seine, a river dividing the city, How sad all can't see this…
what a shame, what a pity.

Then onto the cathedrals, museums and such, Notre-Dame, The Louvre, Arc de Triomphe,
so so much

I'll travel by train, so many stations, there are,

Busily humming to and fro…coming close and then so far.

Do enjoy visiting Paris, France with me, We'll stop at a cafe, order a baguette and tea

I'll explain all of this, in the pages as you read, Just my book and some light is all that you'll need.

Happy Reading

Eiffel Tower

I am in beautiful Paris, France. This city, which is the capital of France, is known as, "The City of Light". The reason that it is called this is because of all of the brilliant illuminated streets and boulevards and structures.

In 1928, Paris lit the Champs-Elysees with gas lamps. (I write about this spectacular street in the next chapter). No other city in Europe did this. There are almost 300 places that light up Paris, hotels, churches, statues, fountains, national buildings and monuments.

Champs-Elysees is a marvelous sight to see· at Christmas time. There are thousands of lights from the Place de la Concorde (a major public square) to the Arc de Triomphe, also 450 decorated trees. On the sidewalk 300 decorated trees are seen and 120 on the pavement.

Of the 37 bridges in Paris, 33 are illuminated at night.

The first place I went to see is the wonderful Eiffel Tower, or "Tour Eiffel", as it is called in Paris. Elevators begin on the ground and stop at three levels. Lots of visitors got off on the second level, which is pretty high up. I wanted to go all the way to the top… I was up 1,050 feet from the ground. A sign at the top said that from that point you could see 45 miles in any direction.

There are over 20,000 sparkling light bulbs that light up this historic structure.

The Eiffel Tower, when built, was the tallest man-made building for 41 years. Then the Chrysler building, built in New York became the tallest for less than a year. In 1931, the Empire State Building, also in New York became the tallest brick building in the world, at 1,250 feet.

Every 7 years, the tower in re-painted to protect it from rust. The French nicknamed it La dame de fer, which means, "the iron lady."

Visitors can climb the stairs to the first two levels, where the are restaurants . Also, they can take the lifts (or elevators) to the third and highest level which is the observation level.

There was a very exciting movie that was made in 1949 called "Man on the Eiffel Tower". The scenes around and in the lifts were very interesting and well done.

When I went back down, I read all about Mr. Gustave Eiffel, who designed it for the Universal Exposition of 1889. It was supposed to be torn down in 1909. Because of the invention of the wireless, transatlantic wireless telephones were operated from the 1,056- foot tower.

Many people were gathered around me reading and looking at all the pictures that are on display about the magnificent "Tour Eiffel".

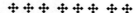

Champs-Élysées

The Champs-Elysees, (pronounced Chan-za-le-za), is one of the most beautiful and legendary promenades, or walk-ways in the world. As I strolled along I was surprised as to how wide the avenue is and found out, stretches for more than two miles.

The Champs-Elysees is lined with chestnut trees, shops, many cafes and cinemas, or theatres. It is perfect for strolling and window-shoppin g. I sipped on a delicious "Orangena" while I people-watched and was intime to see the Normandy Day Parade. American flags were flying everywhere!

I met two lovely sisters as I sat in this chic cafe, watching the beautiful people of Paris scurrying here and there. Rosemary was from California and her sister, Diane was from Ohio. Both are artists and decided to make the trip together to see the city of their dreams and be in the place where so many famous artists lived and displayed their paintings. The girls allowed me to take a picture of them while enjoying the moment.

There is so much to take in on Champs-Elysees, the shopping, art, cozy bistros, intellectuals, flower stands, and the many pastry displays that one cannot pass up. It's a must to buy a delicious bit of French pastry.

The works of many great artists began right here in Paris. Monet, Renoir, Manet, and Degas, just to name a few. It is so nice to be able to read about these master painters on the internet, and see the originals as well as reproductions of their work in many museums and shops in the world.

We sat under some trees that offered visitors a little shade from the heat of the day. I wanted to see more, so I said goodbye to the two sisters and suggested we meet again, perhaps at the Louvre.

As I walked on, I saw the Arc De Triomphe, one of the most famous monuments in Paris. It is 165 feet high and 148 feet wide. It was built between 1806 and 1836 in honor of Napoleon Bonaparte's victories. Napoleon was a French military leader in the 1800's.

The Romans inspired Napoleon to build the 19th- century arch as a tribute to his "Grande Armee." By the early 1960's, the monument became very blackened from coal soot and automobile exhausts. During 1965-1966 it was cleaned by bleaching.

Since I was window-shopping on the Champs-Élysées, I was able to see the wonder of this structure. Then I hailed a cab to get closer but my driver was caught in the swirl of traffic around the base of the building, having a hard time, but we made it.

Beneath the arch is the French Tomb of the Unknown Soldier and a flame that is re-lit every evening at 6:30 p.m.

The only way of reaching the top, I was told, was by climbing the many many steps. There is an elevator, but it is only for the physically challenged. It took a while, but I did it, and saw the magnificent view of the city of Paris from the Arc De Triomphe.

Cathdral of Notre Dame

The Cathedral of Notre Dame was the next place I wanted to visit. It is a sight that no picture could describe.

As I walked through the enormous corridors and past the altars, I thought of the book I read about Napoleon Bonaparte. He was the Emperor of France in 1804-1815. His coronation was held in this very place on December 2, 1804. If you sit very quietly, you can imagine all the splendor of that celebration, with probably hundreds of people attending, and thousands outside standing.

The many statues of bronze, marble and carved wood, are so life-like and I think that only in the Grand Louvre will you see anything to equal the sculptures. There are many coves, or nooks where candles can be lit and one can sit in prayer. The religious statues are so real-like that I had to wonder who were these talented sculptors and artists who performed such amazing works of art.

Looking up, I saw the marvelous stained glass windows. The East and West Rose windows look as if they were painted just a week ago. The truth is that the construction began around 1160. The intricate designs, telling beautiful stories are endless in splendor. I took a picture of the South Rose Window, which measures 19 meters, or over 62 feet across.

Victor Hugo, a great French poet, playwright, novelist and human rights activist said of The Cathedral of Notre-Dame, *"Every wall, every stone of this grand and noble monument is a page not only from the history of France, but also of science and art."* He goes on to say more such as, "each carved image made a contribution to the monument, adding a stone, like great buildings and mountains, are also works of centuries."

I'd like to mention a very good movie that was produced here in this cathedral, is "The Hunchback of Notre-Dame". The book was written by Victor Hugo (who I just wrote about) in 1831. It first was made into a movie in 1923, then several other versions including an animated one.

I spent more time, to attend a Mass at the Cathedral and hear the sounds of the largest organ in all of France. Seven thousand five hundred and forty pipes pour out sounds that are unbelievable!

Ten million tourists every year visit The Cathedral of Notre Dame.

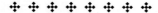

Versailles

Versailles, or Chateau De Versailles, as is called in Paris, was the next place I wanted to visit. The palace is about 13 miles southwest from Paris, which took me about 20 minutes to get there on the wonderful underground train.

This chateaux, or French castle on an estate, is considered the most magnificent in all of France. It is known for the gold leaf, mirrors and absolute power ruled by Louis XIV and his successors. The French Monarchy lived in this "forest of mirrors, gigantic staircases, silk-lined salons, damask curtains and crystal chandeliers.

In 1623, Louis had such joy in hunting, being in the woods and enjoying fresh, fragrant air that he decided to build a pavilion that later was transformed into the structure today known as Versailles.

In 1682, Louis XIV (Louie the 14th), was called the "Sun King" because of the splendor of his court, took the small chateau of Louis III, and enlarged it, really outdoing himself. The huge formal gardens covered 250 acres with 600 fountains, causing a river to be re-directed. Louis XIV had thousands of noblemen plus 9,000 men-at-arms and an equal amount of servants. At any given moment, between 5,000 and 6,000 people were living here at Versailles. Ten thousand courtiers (including 5,000 noblemen) were fed in the court dining rooms every day. They all surrounded the king and served him with dignity. In 1683, the king opened the doors of his apartment and amused them all with games, held dances and spectacles for their amusement.

The estate that enclosed the palace was surrounded by a 25 mile-long wall. This wall had 24 impressive gates. Today, only five of the gates remain. The palace and the grounds are still a magnificent sight to see.

In 1837, the Chamber of Deputies declared Versailles a museum. Much was restored after damages from World War I. This continued by the French government after 1952.

The area of Versailles covers 1,976 acres; 330,000 plants; 375 windows facing onto the huge gardens; also, 70 gardeners, 200 guards, 12 firemen, and 400 members of the general staff to maintain this palace.

More than 20 rooms, which were the apartments of the daughters and sons, are opened to visitors on certain days of the week.

On designated afternoons, 600 jets of water, in the more than 50 fountains and pools in the park outside the palace, are all turned on. It is a spectacular sight...all this at the Chateau De Versailles.

I followed a tour group and walked along with them. So much can be understood when a guide is telling the story about the history of France. We walked around for at least 4 hours, and I think we could have kept walking much longer to see all that there was to see.

My next agenda is to take more rides on the train system under the city of Paris, and learn more about its history.

Paris Metro

I must tell you about the wonderful train system that runs under the city of Paris. For the entire time that I visited, I think I was able to ride on each of the main train lines. The lines are color-coded which makes it easy and fun to figure out where you are going. Hundreds of people can be seen in each and every station, most being underground. There are 700 trains in the metro.

The Paris Metro is the second-busiest metro in Europe, after Moscow. More than 4 million passengers ride the trains a day, and over one billion in a year. There are 303 stations, 16 lines within a 34 square mile of the city of Paris.

The first line opened on July 19, 1900, during the World's Fair. Work continued on the rail system and it was completed by the 1920's.

The job of tunneling below Paris and beneath the River Seine, (pronounced Sen), which divides it, was an unbelievable undertaking when it began over one hundred years ago, in 1898. It started as a half-blind idea that carried on during floods and fires. Many people lost the lives while working in the tunnels.

After World War II construction fell into a decline for almost fifteen years. Paris once lagged behind other countries as far as public transportation, but now the Metro has around fifteen lines…more than any other subway system in the world.

A tourist must pay attention to the directions displayed at all of the stations. I did not and going back to my hotel one evening, I boarded the wrong train and found myself way on the furthest side of Paris. Thanks to several very nice young people, I was directed to a taxi stand and took a long ride back.

Many people who have experienced the outstanding train system in Paris believe that it is a world within itself.

The Galeries Lafayette

The past week has been wonderful here in Paris. I have seen so many breathtaking places and discovered the history of this marvelous city.

I will make a detailed picture album when I return home, and tell all of my friends about my travel experience.

I must see the fashions of Paris, so, it is time for me to do some shopping. Where better, a Parisian suggested, than The Galeries Lafayette. At this massive department store where every type of designer and brand name can be found, I decided to spend the day. This emporium is said to have the largest shoe department in all of Europe.

In 1895, the location began as a small boutique, before the entire building was purchased a year later. The glass and steel dome as well as the staircases were completed by 1912.

From the latest in design collections, cosmetics, home furnishings, jewelry and perfumes to foods, are available in this 10-story structure. The Lafayette offers a real gourmet journey, presenting foods from all over the world. I am told that the average time to spend here is 2 to 3 hours. There are 14 restaurants, a spa, as well as 2 Chanel perfume booths.

As you step through the entrance, overlooking the floors of merchandise is an enormous glass dome. It is really quite a sight to see. It is said that this great store is equaled to 3 large connecting buildings.

This shopping Mecca hosts a popular free weekly fashion show for visitors. I was able to attend one of the shows and it was really exciting. What a unique shopping experience this was...at The Galeries Lafayette.

The Seine River

The Seine River flows through Paris into the English Channel at Le Havre. It

is 776 km long, which is over 482 miles in length.

There are 37 bridges in Paris and many more over the river outside the city. The average depth today is about 9 ½ meters, over 31 feet.

In the 1800's, it was more shallow, most of the time. Today the depth is controlled and built-up banks are usually filled with water.

In January 1910, there was a lot of flooding throughout Paris. The Seine rose to dangerous levels in 1924, 1955, 1982 and 1999. Over 100,000 pieces of artwork had to be moved out of Paris. Much of the art in Paris is kept underground in storage rooms, and so there were threats of flooding.

Napoleon Bonaparte, who died in 1821, asked in his will to be buried on the banks of the Seine… his wished were not granted.

In the 19th and 20th centuries, dozens of artists produced paintings about the beautiful Seine River in Paris. The dozens upon dozens of pieces of art, and their reproductions, can be seen in museums all over the world as well as retail shops.

I took an amazing river cruise on the Seine that included a 3-course dinner. This was an unforgettable evening, So I leave this beautiful river and go on the cemetery at Pére-Lachaise.

Cimetiére Pére-Lachaise

There is a cemetery at Pére-Lachaise, called Cimetiére Pére-Lachaise and a very interesting place to visit. I read so much about it and where many famous people are buried that I had to make that my next stop.

The city itself is a small one and not famous for anything except this beautiful cemetery in a huge wooded park. It was built on a hill with beautiful views of Paris, and is the largest cemetery in Paris, France. The dim cobble stoned walk-ways are unique, and there are so many mausoleums and grave sites that make it seem like a city in a city. The cemetery was founded in May 21, 1804. As you walk along every path, you cannot help but to stop and stare. There are 110 acres here, making it the largest cemetery in Paris.

There are statues of grieving widows crying, and angels hovering over the graves. Egyptian pyramids and obelisks also have their place in this reverent location. A tomb showing a bronze figure breaking out of the grave is an amazing creation of stone.

Pére-Lachaise is the final resting place for many notable people such as Fredéric Chopin, Oscar Wilde, Edith Piaf, Sarah Bernhardt and Modigliani, who was an Italian painter and sculptor. Movie actors, Yves Montand and his wife Simone Signoret have a beautiful monument there, also the American singer, Jim Morrison of the 1960's rock group "The Doors", is buried here. Visitors leave gift of flowers and other things on his grave which has a guard positioned there so that the gravestone is not damaged.

I found out that if someone wants to be buried in the cemetery, one must die in Paris.

It is said that when Napoleon Bonaparte was Emperor of France, he proclaimed about this cemetery that, *"every citizen has the right to be buried here, regardless of race or religion."*

I went over to the vaults and found where Isadora Duncan was buried in 1927. She was called the "matriarch of modern dance". She forever changed people's ideas of ballet. Her life and death is a very sad story. In 1968, Vanessa Redgrave, acted as her, in the movie titled, "Isadora."

There were cats everywhere in this cemetery. I asked about them and was told that the entire area is a haven for cats and there were hundreds living there. They crawl in and out of the beautiful monuments and seem very much at home.

As I turned a corner, I spotted one of the sisters that I met in the chic café on the Champs-Élysées last week. Rosemary allowed me to snap a picture of her while she was positioning her camera to take one . We spoke for a while, agreeing as to this amazing cemetery, and our plans of meeting up at the Louvre.

I spent many hours at this amazing place, totally losing time. Being here gives you a strange but peaceful feeling…but now it was time to leave, leave this little city with the breath-taking cemetery, and the memories that live on in this spiritual burial ground.

Louvre Museum

Well I sure can't leave Paris until I visit the Louvre Museum. It is a historic monument and one of the world's largest museums, located on the Right Bank of the Seine in the 1st district, called an arrondissement.

There are more than 35,000 objects to see from prehistoric times up to the 21st century. All of these items are in exhibit over more than 652,000 square feet. More than 10 million people visit this amazing museum each year.

The opening of the Louvre was August 10, 1793 and had about 500 paintings. There were building problems and so the doors were closed in

1796 until 1801. Thousands of pieces were added, but during World War II, the museum removed most of the art and hid valuable pieces. The beginning of 1945, after the liberation of France, art was beginning to return to the Louvre.

In 1983, the French president had plans to renovate the building, allowing the displays all through the building, and an architect was given the job of designing a glass pyramid to stand over the new entrance in the main court. This pyramid and its underground lobby were introduced on October 15, 1988, then completed in 1989. As of 2002, the attendance doubled since the completion of the pyramid.

Since my next plan to visit was Egypt, I went to see the Egyptian department. There are over 50,000 pieces including many things from the Nile that date back from 4,000BC to the 4th century. The collection can be found in more than 20 rooms. These include art, papyrus scrolls, mummies, tools, clothing, jewelry, games, musical instruments, and weapons.

Sisters, Rosemary and Diane, found me browsing around the incredible Egyptian area. They said they figured I'd be there because I mentioned that Egypt would be my next travel destination.

After hours of walking and viewing, we found a very nice balcony to relax and have some tea. The panoramic view from there was unbelievable. I tried to take a picture of the guests enjoying the service and the statues...oh, the statues.

There are so many more museums and restaurants here in Paris, but it is difficult to visit them all in a short vacation. I do plan on returning someday to take in more of the beautiful sights.

I still had a day left before returning home, so I will go to the Sacré-Coeur. It is said that some point, every visitor to Paris arrives at this beautiful church.

Sacré-Coeur

There is a hill in Paris, a hill with a very long flight of steps overlooking rooftops of the city. It is where the Paris, of many years ago thrived with artists, displaying beautiful paintings and Parisians busy with their daily routine. It is Montmartre. This area produced so many amazing artists and memorable contributions to the world, that one wants to walk through the legendary region just to whisper to yourself, "I am here." At the top of this flight of steps is a magnificent church called the Church of the Sacré-Coeur (or sacred heart).

The basilica stands on the hill of Montmartre, and has been a sacred site since pagan times. This locality has a confusing history, from the Middle Ages and French Revolution, but is now a major cultural center in this vicinity.

The construction of the Sacré-Coeur is primarily stone from a quarry that is known for its high content of calcite. When the weather is damp, calcite seeps out of the stone which then keeps the appearance of the monument to be chalky-white.

The top of the dome is open to the public. This point is the second-highest point in Paris, after the Eiffel Tower, and is 271 feet above Montmartre. The dome is supported by 80 columns. Tourists visit the church just for the panoramic view. When plans were being made for the basilica, there were so many delays, due to laws, when finally the foundation stone was laid on June 16, 1875. There were additional situations in the way of the final construction, but attempts to halt the construction was defeated in 1897, by that time the interior was complete and open for services.

As I entered the door of the basilica, I was surprised at how dim and gloomy it was. Only the brilliance of the golden mosaics glowing on the altar could be seen.

There is an entrance to the crypt, but I did not care to see the area. The Crypt contains statues of saints and relics. Many rumors have been told as to what the relics really are, or the history behind what are in the urns and containers. As I saw the entrance, I saw Rosemary sitting down and feeding the pigeons and doves. She said her sister, Diane was taking a nap.

In the relic chapel, there is an urn on the left that is said to contain the heart of the minister who wrote the law to the public utility department that allowed the land at the top of Montmartre to be taken for the basilica.

The basilica complex has a lovely garden for meditation, with a fountain. This was my last view of the Sacré-Coeur, and the end to my wonderful adventures in Paris France.

I've enjoyed every minute that I spent here, and am grateful for the friends that I met. People are beautiful here in France, and though many do speak the English language, they seem to really appreciate when tourists try to speak French. Visiting other countries and cultures brings the world together just a bit more. With so much unrest and unhappiness in the world, it is very refreshing to know that other countries do enjoy tourists who want to see and understand their way of life.

So, I am getting a cab and heading for the airport…farewell to this beautiful city of Paris, France. I hope you enjoyed reading about my journey.